TENNESSEE TITANS

LUKE HANLON

WWW.APEXEDITIONS.COM

Copyright © 2025 by Apex Editions, Mendota Heights, MN 55120. All rights reserved. No part of this book may be reproduced or utilized in any form or by any means without written permission from the publisher.

Apex is distributed by North Star Editions:
sales@northstareditions.com | 888-417-0195

Produced for Apex by Red Line Editorial.

Photographs ©: Kirk Irwin/AP Images, cover, 1; Andy Lyons/Getty Images Sport/Getty Images, 4–5; George Walker IV/AP Images, 6–7; Gordon Peters/San Francisco Chronicle/AP Images, 8–9; David F. Smith/AP Images, 10–11; Michael Zagaris/Getty Images Sport/Getty Images, 12–13; Harry Cabluck/AP Images, 14–15; David Longsreath/AP Images, 16–17; Anthony Neste/Getty Images Sport/Getty Images, 19; AP Images, 20–21, 22–23; Ed Kolenovsky/AP Images, 24–25; George Gojkovich/Getty Images Sport/Getty Images, 26–27; Focus On Sport/Getty Images Sport/Getty Images, 29; Randy Piland/The Tennessean/AP Images, 30–31, 58–59; Mike Zarrilli/Getty Images Sport/Getty Images, 32–33; Matt Sullivan/Getty Images Sport/Getty Images, 34–35; Kathryn Riley/Getty Images Sport/Getty Images, 36–37; G. Newman Lowrance/AP Images, 38–39; Elsa/Getty Images Sport/Getty Images, 40–41; Jonathan Ferrey/Getty Images Sport/Getty Images, 42–43; Justin Ford/Getty Images Sport/Getty Images, 44–45; Paul Spinelli/AP Images, 47, 57; Brett Carlsen/Getty Images Sport/Getty Images, 48–49; Shutterstock Images, 50–51; Carmen Mandato/Getty Images Sport/Getty Images, 52–53; Wade Payne/AP Images, 54–55

Library of Congress Control Number: 2024911561

ISBN
979-8-89250-161-3 (hardcover)
979-8-89250-178-1 (paperback)
979-8-89250-302-0 (ebook pdf)
979-8-89250-195-8 (hosted ebook)

Printed in the United States of America
Mankato, MN
012025

NOTE TO PARENTS AND EDUCATORS
Apex books are designed to build literacy skills in striving readers. Exciting, high-interest content attracts and holds readers' attention. The text is carefully leveled to allow students to achieve success quickly.

TABLE OF CONTENTS

CHAPTER 1
TITAN UP! 4

CHAPTER 2
EARLY HISTORY 8

PLAYER SPOTLIGHT
EARL CAMPBELL 18

CHAPTER 3
LEGENDS 20

PLAYER SPOTLIGHT
WARREN MOON 28

CHAPTER 4
RECENT HISTORY 30

CHAPTER 5
MODERN STARS 38

PLAYER SPOTLIGHT
DERRICK HENRY 46

CHAPTER 6
TEAM TRIVIA 48

TEAM RECORDS • 56
TIMELINE • 58
COMPREHENSION QUESTIONS • 60
GLOSSARY • 62
TO LEARN MORE • 63
ABOUT THE AUTHOR • 63
INDEX • 64

CHAPTER 1

TITAN UP!

Thousands of fans rise from their seats. They are in Nashville, Tennessee. The city is known for country music. A country artist sings the national anthem. Then the Tennessee Titans take the field.

Quarterback Will Levis runs out onto the field before a 2023 game.

Jeffery Simmons had five solo tackles and a sack in a 2023 game against the Carolina Panthers.

The Titans play a physical style of football. For example, Jeffery Simmons leads the defense. He doesn't avoid blockers. He runs through them. Then he delivers a powerful tackle. Fans hope the Titans can bruise their way to a victory.

TOUGH TITANS

Tennessee's slogan is "Titan Up!" For many fans, it is a play on words. It sounds the same as "tighten up." The slogan can stand for a few things. One is staying focused. One is toughness. Another is playing to win.

CHAPTER 2

EARLY HISTORY

The Tennessee Titans started out as the Houston Oilers. They played their first season in 1960. They were part of the AFL. This league was separate from the NFL. The Oilers were stacked with offensive talent.

The Houston Oilers (white jerseys) won their first-ever game 37–22.

The Oilers won the AFL title in their first season. They beat the Los Angeles Chargers. The next season's AFL title game was a rematch. The Oilers defense stepped up. They held the Chargers to three points. The Oilers were champs again.

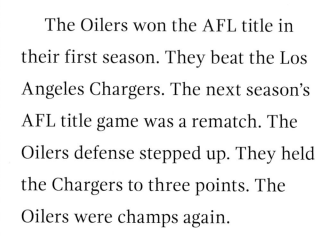

OVERTIME THRILLER

The 1962 AFL championship featured the Oilers for the third straight time. This time they played the Dallas Texans. The Oilers were losing 17–0. But they came back. They forced overtime. However, the Texans won with a field goal in double overtime.

Billy Cannon (20) scores a touchdown in the 1961 AFL title game.

The early success didn't last in Houston. During the rest of the 1960s, the Oilers made the playoffs only twice. In 1970, the AFL joined the NFL. The move didn't help the Oilers. But a new coach did. Bum Phillips took over in 1975. He fit in with Houston. He often wore a cowboy hat and boots.

LUV YA BLUE

The Oilers were famous for their light-blue jerseys. In 1979, an Oilers fan hung up a sign at Houston's practice field. The sign said, "Luv Ya Blue." Soon, those signs became common. And the saying became the team's slogan.

Bum Phillips (right) talks with a player during a 1975 game.

In 1978, Phillips led the Oilers back to the playoffs. They made it all the way to the conference championship game. However, the Oilers fell to the Pittsburgh Steelers. The next year, the Oilers made it back to the championship game. But once again, the Steelers came out on top.

WARM WELCOME

Fans are usually sad or angry when their team loses. But Houston fans were proud in 1978 and 1979. They showed their pride after both playoff losses in Pittsburgh. At the team's stadium, people welcomed the team home.

Cold rain made the 1978 season's conference title game wet and slippery.

Houston reached the playoffs again in 1980. But the team lost in the first round. After that, the Oilers fired Phillips. Fans were furious.
The Oilers struggled afterward, too. They missed the playoffs for six years straight. Then things turned around. Starting in 1987, the team made the playoffs seven years in a row. But the Oilers never got close to the Super Bowl. Then they had a tough season in 1996. It was time for a big change.

Haywood Jeffires helped the Oilers go 11–5 in 1991. His 100 catches that season led the NFL.

PLAYER SPOTLIGHT

EARL CAMPBELL

Football fans in Texas had long cheered for Earl Campbell. He played high school football in Tyler, Texas. Then he stayed in Texas for college. Campbell became the clear No. 1 pick in the 1978 draft. The Oilers selected him.

Campbell took the NFL by storm. In his first season, he led the league in rushing yards. He did it again the next two years. Campbell used his 232-pound (105-kg) frame to punish defenders. He was key to the Oilers' playoff runs in 1978 and 1979.

EARL CAMPBELL WAS NAMED OFFENSIVE PLAYER OF THE YEAR IN EACH OF HIS FIRST THREE SEASONS.

CHAPTER 3

LEGENDS

Quarterback George Blanda was the first Oilers star. He led the team to AFL titles in 1960 and 1961. Blanda threw for 3,330 yards in 1961. He also tossed 36 touchdown passes. Both of those numbers led the league. Blanda had a powerful leg, too. He kicked long field goals with ease.

George Blanda (16) watches his pass during a 1965 game against the New York Jets.

Ken Houston racked up interceptions with the Oilers. The safety was dangerous once he had the ball, too. He returned nine interceptions for touchdowns. When he retired, that was the most touchdowns by a defensive player.

Defensive lineman Elvin Bethea excelled at rushing the passer. He dodged blockers with his agility. Then he tackled with great force. Bethea's 105 sacks are the most in team history.

Ken Houston had 25 interceptions in his six years with the Oilers.

PICKS AND KICKS

Jim Norton was another great Oilers defender. He intercepted 45 passes in nine seasons. That was a team record. But Norton did more than play safety. He was also one of the best punters in the league.

Robert Brazile was one of the best defensive players of his time. The linebacker earned the nickname "Dr. Doom." He was known for his hard hits. Brazile was also tough. In 10 seasons, he never missed a game. He retired in 1984. Ray Childress began his career the next year. Childress soon became a top defensive lineman. He forced many fumbles.

ASTRODOME

The Astrodome opened in 1965. The stadium was built for baseball. It hosted the Houston Astros. But the Oilers started playing there in 1968. The Astrodome became the first domed stadium in pro football.

From 1976 to 1982, Robert Brazile (52) made seven straight Pro Bowls.

Ernest Givins catches a pass during a 1993 game.

Earl Campbell was a dominant running back for Houston. He won the Most Valuable Player (MVP) Award in 1979. Quarterback Warren Moon began his Oilers career in 1984. Moon topped 4,600 passing yards in 1990. He did it again the next year. In both of those seasons, he led the NFL in passing yards.

RELIABLE RECEIVER

Warren Moon's favorite target was Ernest Givins. The wide receiver spent nine years with Houston. In eight of those seasons, he recorded more than 700 yards. In 1992, Givins nabbed 10 touchdown catches.

PLAYER SPOTLIGHT

WARREN MOON

Warren Moon had a great college career. But NFL teams didn't want him. Many white owners and coaches held racist beliefs. They thought Black people couldn't succeed at quarterback. So, Moon played in the Canadian Football League. He won five straight titles there. NFL teams stopped ignoring him.

The Oilers signed Moon in 1984. Over the next 10 years, he piled up more than 33,000 passing yards. In 2006, Moon became the first Black quarterback in the Pro Football Hall of Fame.

WARREN MOON MADE THE PRO BOWL IN SIX OF HIS TEN SEASONS WITH THE OILERS.

CHAPTER 4
RECENT HISTORY

The team's owner wanted a new stadium. The city of Houston wouldn't build one, though. So in 1997, the Oilers moved to Tennessee. They didn't have their own stadium at first. But after two years, they got one in Nashville.

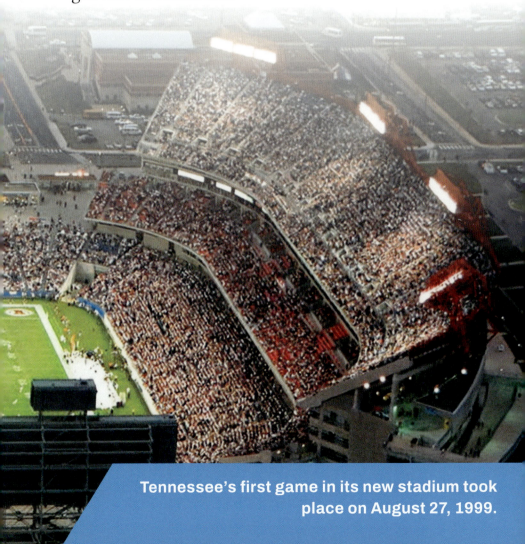

Tennessee's first game in its new stadium took place on August 27, 1999.

The Oilers changed their name to the Titans in 1999. That season, the Titans made it all the way to the Super Bowl. They faced the St. Louis Rams. With six seconds left, the Titans trailed by seven. Tennessee wide receiver Kevin Dyson caught a pass at the 5-yard line. But he was tackled one yard short of the end zone. The Rams won.

Kevin Dyson (87) comes up one yard short in the Tennessee Titans' Super Bowl loss.

MUSIC CITY MIRACLE

Tennessee's 1999 playoff run started against the Buffalo Bills. The Titans were down 16–15 with 16 seconds left. They received a kickoff. Then Frank Wycheck threw a lateral pass. Kevin Dyson caught it and ran. He returned the kick for the game-winning touchdown. The play soon became known as "The Music City Miracle."

Running back Chris Johnson (28) led the Titans' ground game from 2008 to 2013.

The Titans remained contenders for several years. Head coach Jeff Fisher played a big role. He coached the team for 17 seasons. In six of those seasons, the Titans won at least 10 games. However, the team fired Fisher in 2011. After that, Tennessee struggled.

PASSING TO YOURSELF

In the 2017 season, the Titans reached the playoffs for the first time in years. At halftime, the Kansas City Chiefs led 21–3. But the second half was different. Titans quarterback Marcus Mariota threw a pass. A Chiefs defender swatted the ball. It bounced back to Mariota. He caught it and scored a touchdown. Tennessee came back to win the game.

Mike Vrabel became Tennessee's head coach in 2018. The next season, the Titans pulled off two upsets in the playoffs. They reached the conference title game. But they lost to Kansas City. After that, the Titans won their division two years in a row.

In 2023, rookie Will Levis took over at quarterback. And in 2024, Brian Callahan took over as head coach. Fans remained hopeful that the Titans would soon return to the Super Bowl.

In 2019, the Titans defeated the New England Patriots in the first round of the playoffs.

CHAPTER 5

MODERN STARS

Eddie George started his career in 1996 with the Houston Oilers. The running back followed the team to Tennessee. He stayed through the 2003 season. George never missed a game with the team. He ran for more than 1,000 yards in seven different seasons.

Eddie George's best year came in 2000. He topped 1,500 rushing yards that season.

Steve McNair (9) threw 24 touchdown passes in 2003.

George often relied on Bruce Matthews to open up running lanes. The offensive lineman made 14 straight Pro Bowls. Matthews also protected quarterback Steve McNair until 2001. McNair truly shined in 2003. His strong arm and ability to scramble came together. He was one of two co-MVPs that season.

SPEED MACHINE

Chris Johnson joined the Titans in 2008. He used his elite speed to bust long runs. In 2009, the running back gained more than 2,000 yards on the ground. Only five players had done that before.

Keith Bulluck (53) made more than 1,000 tackles in his decade as a Titan.

The Titans had a strong defense for much of the 2000s. Keith Bulluck shut down the middle of the field. The linebacker flew around to make tackles. In front of Bulluck was Albert Haynesworth. The defensive lineman weighed 335 pounds (152 kg). It often took more than one offensive lineman to block him.

THE FREAK

Defensive lineman Jevon Kearse was dominant in 1999 as a rookie. "The Freak" had 14.5 sacks in his first season. He also forced eight fumbles. That led the league. Kearse's best years came as a Titan.

Derrick Henry's career got off to a slow start. But by 2018, he was one of the best running backs in the NFL. He proved it with a 99-yard touchdown run that season. He led the league in rushing in 2019 and 2020.

Like Henry, Ryan Tannehill had a rough start to his career. Then the Titans traded for the quarterback in 2019. Tannehill's play turned around. He led the Titans to three straight playoff appearances.

Ryan Tannehill passes the ball during a 2022 game against the New York Giants.

PLAYER SPOTLIGHT

DERRICK HENRY

Derrick Henry was big for a running back. He stood 6-foot-3 (191 cm). And he weighed 247 pounds (112 kg). That's as large as some defensive linemen. But Henry was also one of the fastest players on the field.

Henry's size and speed made him hard to tackle. He could run over defenders. Or he could run past them. Sometimes he even jumped over them. This combination of skills helped Henry run for 2,027 yards in 2020. He was just the eighth player to rush for more than 2,000 yards in a season.

DERRICK HENRY EARNED HIS FOURTH PRO BOWL NOD IN 2023.

CHAPTER 6
TEAM TRIVIA

Nashville is known as "Music City." Country singer Johnny Cash is especially popular there. Titans fans hear him before the fourth quarter of home games. "Folsom Prison Blues" plays in the stadium.

Country star Trace Adkins has sung the national anthem before multiple Titans games.

The Titans' logo has three stars, similar to Tennessee's state flag.

The Titans got their team name because of Nashville. The city is often called "The Athens of the South." Athens is a city in Greece. Titans are creatures in Greek mythology. The team's logo is based on ancient Greece, too. For example, flames surround the T. Fire is a key part of Greek myths.

A TEAM FOR TENNESSEE

The Titans don't have Nashville in their team name. The team's owner wanted the Titans to represent the entire state. That's why there are three red stars in the team's logo. They stand for East, West, and Middle Tennessee.

Entering 2024, the Titans and Texans had played 44 times. The Titans had won 23 of those games.

Houston got a new NFL team in 2002. Since then, the Houston Texans and the Titans have been rivals. Houston fans don't like the Titans because the team left their city. Players have even fought during games.

TITANS-JAGUARS RIVALRY

In 1999, a rivalry started between the Titans and the Jacksonville Jaguars. The Jaguars finished that season 14–2. Their only losses were to the Titans. Then the Titans beat the Jaguars in the playoffs as well.

The team took a few years to get settled in Tennessee. In 1997, games took place in Memphis. Games moved to Nashville in 1998. But they were at a college stadium. The Titans' stadium opened the next year. It can hold more than 69,000 fans.

SUPER FANS

The Titans have dozens of super fans. Some dress up as titans when they go to games. Others wear flames on their heads. One super fan is called "The Collector." He owns hundreds of Titans jerseys and other items.

Fans wear all sorts of gear to show their love of the Titans.

TEAM RECORDS

All-Time Passing Yards: 33,685
Warren Moon (1984–93)

All-Time Touchdown Passes: 196
Warren Moon (1984–93)

All-Time Rushing Yards: 10,009
Eddie George (1996–2003)

All-Time Rushing Touchdowns: 90
Derrick Henry (2016–23)

All-Time Receiving Yards: 7,935
Ernest Givins (1986–94)

All-Time Interceptions: 45
Jim Norton (1960–68)

All-Time Sacks: 105*
Elvin Bethea (1968–83)

All-Time Scoring: 1,060
Al Del Greco (1991–2000)

All-Time Coaching Wins: 142
Jeff Fisher (1994–2010)

AFL Titles: 2
(1960, 1961)

Sacks were not an official statistic until 1982. However, researchers have studied old games to determine sacks dating back to 1960.

All statistics are accurate through 2023.

TIMELINE

1960 — The Houston Oilers play their first season and win the AFL championship.

1961 — The Oilers win their second straight AFL title.

1970 — The Oilers join the NFL after the league joins together with the AFL.

1975 — The Oilers hire Bum Phillips to be the team's head coach.

1978 — Phillips leads the Oilers to the playoffs for the first time in nine years.

1980 | **1994** | **1996** | **1999** | **2019**

Jeff Fisher becomes the Oilers' head coach.

The team becomes the Titans and reaches the Super Bowl for the first time.

The Oilers fire Phillips after they lose in the playoffs for the third straight year.

The Oilers play their last season in Houston before moving to Tennessee.

The Titans reach the conference championship game for the first time since 2002.

59

COMPREHENSION QUESTIONS

Write your answers on a separate piece of paper.

1. Write a paragraph that explains the main ideas of Chapter 4.

2. Who do you think was the greatest player in Titans history? Why?

3. Which running back did the Oilers select with the top pick in 1978?
   - A. Earl Campbell
   - B. Eddie George
   - C. Derrick Henry

4. How does the Titans' logo represent all of Tennessee, and not just Nashville?
   - A. The flames stand for the state's wildfires.
   - B. The logo is in the shape of the state.
   - C. The three stars stand for each part of the state.

5. What does **agility** mean in this book?

*Defensive lineman Elvin Bethea excelled at rushing the passer. He dodged blockers with his **agility**.*

    A. strength
    B. quickness
    C. size

6. What does **rookie** mean in this book?

*Defensive lineman Jevon Kearse was dominant in 1999 as a **rookie**. "The Freak" had 14.5 sacks in his first season.*

    A. a player in his last season
    B. an athlete no longer playing
    C. a player in his first season

Answer key on page 64.

GLOSSARY

conference
A group of teams that make up part of a sports league.

division
In the NFL, a group of teams that make up part of a conference.

draft
A system that lets teams select new players coming into the league.

fumbles
When players lose control of the ball.

interceptions
Passes that are caught by a defensive player.

lateral pass
A pass that goes sideways or backward.

overtime
An extra period that happens if two teams are tied at the end of the fourth quarter.

sacks
Plays that happen when a defender tackles the quarterback before he can throw the ball.

scramble
When a quarterback runs to avoid pass rushers.

upsets
Games won by a team that was expected to lose.

TO LEARN MORE

BOOKS

Anderson, Josh. *Tennessee Titans*. Mankato, MN: The Child's World, 2022.

Blue, Tyler. *Stars of the NFL*. New York: Abbeville Kids, 2023.

Coleman, Ted. *Tennessee Titans All-Time Greats*. Mendota Heights, MN: Press Box Books, 2022.

ONLINE RESOURCES

Visit **www.apexeditions.com** to find links and resources related to this title.

ABOUT THE AUTHOR

Luke Hanlon is a sportswriter, editor, and author based in Minneapolis. He watches NFL games all day on Sundays during the fall.

INDEX

Bethea, Elvin, 22
Blanda, George, 21
Brazile, Robert, 24
Bulluck, Keith, 43

Callahan, Brian, 36
Campbell, Earl, 18, 27
Childress, Ray, 24

Dyson, Kevin, 32–33

Fisher, Jeff, 35

George, Eddie, 38, 41
Givins, Ernest, 27

Haynesworth, Albert, 43
Henry, Derrick, 44, 46
Houston, Ken, 22

Johnson, Chris, 41

Kearse, Jevon, 43

Levis, Will, 36

Mariota, Marcus, 35
Matthews, Bruce, 41
McNair, Steve, 41
Moon, Warren, 27, 28

Norton, Jim, 23

Phillips, Bum, 12, 14, 16

Simmons, Jeffery, 7
Super Bowl, 16, 32, 36

Tannehill, Ryan, 44

Vrabel, Mike, 36

Wycheck, Frank, 33

ANSWER KEY:
1. Answers will vary; 2. Answers will vary; 3. A; 4. C; 5. B; 6. C